Chocolate *and* Cigarettes

Chocolate *and* Cigarettes

Volume VII
2013-2014

Arthur R. Marinello

Copyright @2015 by Arthur R. Marinello

Published by Rivershore Books

ISBN: 978-0692500095

All rights reserved. No part of this book may be reproduced or transmitted in any form or by any means, electronic or mechanical, including photocopying, recording, or by any information storage and retrieval system, without permission in writing from the copyright owner.

This book was printed in the United States of America.

Preface

As I've been lately seeking for an appropriate preface for this book I thought to look through its contents for a guide, when, even before I took a look, I realized that the tendency on my part is to point out the transitional nature of life. There is constant changing in our world and that, actually, transitioning, changing, is the name of the game. And somehow, we must both acknowledge this as well as try to deal with it. And I hope that these lines perform a service in that regard.

A.R.M.
July 17, 2015

Table of Contents

1.	You Tell Me	1
2.	Clueless	2
3.	An Adventure	3
4.	So Be It	4
5.	There are Variations	5
6.	It's a Miracle	7
7.	I Confuse	8
8.	Not Really	9
9.	Not a Care in the World	11
10.	Early this Morning	12
11.	A Guiding Force	18
12.	The Weather	20
13.	In the Same Boat	21
14.	Control	22
15.	Counterproductive	23
16.	The Young	24
17.	It Feels Right	25
18.	He Doesn't Belong	27
19.	The Incompetency of Leadership	29
20.	Challenges	33
21.	Glory	34
22.	God!	35
23.	Paul's Heaven	38
24.	If Then	39
25.	The Gnawing	40
26.	Chocolate and Cigarettes	43
27.	Psychoanalysis	47
28.	Jerry	48
29.	Crazy	49
30.	That's the Story	52
31.	Leo, Leo	56
32.	What I Have Done	59
33.	A Pigeon	60
34.	There's a Certain	61
35.	That's How I Would Have Done It	62
36.	Learning	65
37.	Father Martin	66
38.	Islam	70

39.	Heroically	72
40.	Will I?	74
41.	Mine	75
42.	Our Little Acre	76
43.	The Other Day	77
44.	The Tribunal	79
45.	Disguises	82
46.	The Eternal	83
47.	A Form of Expression	84
48.	Underlying	85
49.	An Inner Force	86
50.	The Chess Board	88
51.	This is Too Much	89
52.	Misfittings	91
53.	You Know	93
54.	God Loves You	96
55.	Overwork	99

You Tell Me

8:22 a.m. Saturday
June 1, 2013

It's hard to look
At this eighty five year
Old woman

And see an eighty five
Year old woman

Despite the aches and pains
And sixty five years
Of marriage

And all the experiences
We've been through
Together

I see the eighteen year old
I first saw
Cross the front
Of the room
That psych class
At Brooklyn College
Eons ago

You tell me

Clueless

8:28 am Saturday
June 1, 2013

I don't mean to complain
Life has its way
There are so many imponderables

But really,
These younger generations.

Clueless

On a different track
A totally different track

Limping along
Careening

Sometimes it's frightening

Wherefore?

How?

An Adventure

10:02 am Thursday
June 13, 2013

It is simple really
Look upon it as an
Adventure

Crossing the street
Yes

In times past
In the war
There were times when you were
Strafed
Bombed
Shelled
Buzz bombed

You didn't give it much thought

So now, you have trouble
Crossing the street
Standing up
For a while

Do not despair
Look on it all
As an adventure

So Be It

10:23 am Thursday
June 27, 2013

It's all right
It's all right
Because it has to be

People have different opinions
That's how we're made

But it's disturbing
And confusing

Some of these opinions
And lifestyles
Are disturbing
And confusing

They can be way off the mark
Some, never the less,
Hold sway

They gain credence
That have none

So be it

There are Variations

8:15 Saturday
June 29, 2013

We are all of us different
And for every difference
There are variations

No one is one hundred percent
Normal
Or obese
Schizophrenic
Intelligent
Feeble minded
Or whatever

We must rid ourselves
Of the strait jacketed
One size fits all

Why?

Because it's inaccurate

And in so being
Does an injustice
To many
Or even most
In the category
Being considered

New Orleans, stationary figure

It's a Miracle

7:55 am Wednesday
July 3, 2013

It's been hot lately
Southern California hot

Four or five days
In the hundreds

As high as 107°

Today, there is a change
Cool air is blowing in
Probably lifted
From the ocean
Twenty or thirty miles way

It feels like a miracle
It is a miracle

We may have an idea
Of how it works

That doesn't make it any less
A miracle

To me

I Confuse

8:40 am Tuesday
July 30, 2013

I confuse my family
I'm healthy
Within various parameters

I'm healthy
Up to a point

And my family
With variations
Feel I can continue
Doing things
I used to do

I'm reasonably alert
And that probably
Causes the confusion

But I'm old
 And rather feeble
I'm ninety three

And it's rather comical
For people to opine
On what it's like to be
Ninety three
Who are so much
Younger

Not Really

8:50 am Tuesday
Juley 30, 2013

I'm Italian
Though not really
I was born in New York City
And have lived my life
As an American

I'm Italian
Though not really
I'm not Roman
Or Milanese
Or Venetian

I'm Italian
Though not really
I'm part Sicilian
And part Neapolitan
And like such people
I'm different

As such
I'm not very much
Like a German
Or a Frenchman
Or an Englishman

Mom and Geri

Mom and Pop, 1936, Prospect Park

Not a Care in the World

2:50 pm Tuesday
August 13, 2013

Here it is
2:30 pm
On a hot August afternoon
In Sunny Southern California
98° in the garage
I've just returned from Staples
Buying something like a chip
A memory thing
For a recording device
My son-in-law, Larry, gave me
So that I would record
Some of my poetry

And I look out
On my backyard
And, as usual
Wonder how I came to be here
Sixty five years in Southern California
No less
Ever wondering

And so, I thought
Could I transform myself
Into that young lad in Brooklyn
Mom was here
Pop was there
And I hadn't a care in the world

Early this Morning

4:21 pm Wednesday
Sept. 4, 2013

Early this morning
A few hours ago
As I was sitting in my library
The opening of the front door
Was an indication
That my wife was returned
From eight o'clock mass

And I asked her to join me
To sit beside me
And she came,
In tears

Leo is dying, she said
Terry had told her
And he would be moving
Into hospice
He was dying

He was dying
And she had to go there
To be with Elsie

I was not eager
To see her go
The temperature has been
In the hundreds
And still was

I was able to prevail upon her
To delay going
Might she not go to the market,
El Super,
And see how things were
In an hour or so?
And she did

After a while
I decided to call Elsie
Which I did
After eight rings
I gave up

She called back
She told me how dire
The situation was
It's very bad, she said
And I told her
That Vera had been planning
To come
To the hospital
And she was appreciative
And maybe
She misunderstood me
When she said
I'll see you, Art
I had not planned on going
We're all of us
Pretty old
You know
But I was stuck
So, in due time, we left
Unbearably hot

As we came near Leo's room
We found a number of people there
Waiting to be let into Leo's room

Elsie, Mario, Barbara, Steve
And we waited,
Together
And then we were let in

Leo lay there
Tubes in his nose
And something attached
To his right ear
And it was bothering him
He tried to reach that ear
With his left hand
To no avail
He couldn't
And he was dying
Eyes closed
No matter
For the past few years when I
     would greet him
         all I would get
            was an empty stare
               a vacant empty stare
He was not there

And so, I thought,
He's dying
There's nothing left
What do I have to lose
There's really nothing to lose
Or, was it not a thought
But a feeling

And I began talking
Certainly loudly enough
Standing by his hospital bed
Of the time we had come
The four of us
To Costa del Sol
Arising the next morning
Leo and I
To proceed to the beach
Where we had been told
The women would be topless

There was a drizzle
Which did not deter us,
After all

The beach was deserted
No one there
And Leo and I,
Disappointed,
Went back to our hotel

And as I spoke in the hospital room
Of this twenty four year ago
    incident
A first – stage miracle occurred
Leo opened his eyes
His beautiful blue eyes
And life was in them

And I continued
The day in Madrid when we came
    upon the most dangerous –
    looking people I'd ever seen
And the canes we each bought
With eagle's heads
And Father Emory Tang's strident answer
    To a question about when
        The church would have
        women priests
"When God says so"
And Leo smiled, the first I'd seen
    in years
And his eyes were open
And he tried to talk
Well, all well and good
This was surely a miracle
A gift
And certainly sufficient
    You could say
To make up for the years, without

And you would be right
But who are you –
Who am I, to say

As Barbara tried
On the other side of his bed
To relieve the discomfort
      he was feeling,
He looked at her
A look with such expression
      in those blue eyes
So filled with tenderness
      That is beyond imagining

It was as if God was in them
    Or his holy angels
      Or the Virgin
Expression had returned to them
Leo was back
For however long
And those who were there
Who could witness
Could experience
Were receiving
A blessing

A Guiding Force

9:45 Friday
Sept 6, 2013

It seems to me
That women are superior
Superior to men, that is

They are,
Generally speaking
Disinclined to kill
Whereas men are

Women are focused
On nurturing
On the gentle way

And besides
They are so attractive
Beautiful, in fact

And they are skilled
In human relations
And they often act
As a guiding force

They do a lot of the managing
Of human activities
A guiding force

The Catholic Church itself,
Would be hard pressed
To function without women
Women are the back bone
    of the church
As they are of so many other
    facets of life

As for men
    Men have been given some
        of the qualities to round out
           the mission of this
              human race
Men, have been endowed
    with intellectual
      force sometimes
And physical strength
And physical courage
And necessariness

God, in his wisdom, and as
    an afterthought,
        did try to establish
        a balance
But never did he tip the
    balance in favor
        of men

The Weather

3:55 pm Friday
Sept. 6, 2013

The weather is like a peach tree
Here it is
Temperature in the hundreds
For weeks now

And we wait
Wait for it to be better
Waiting for temperatures
To go down
To the eighties maybe
Waiting

And the peach trees
We waited
The buds came
Then the tiny peaches
And then the ripening

And, finally,
The mature,
The edible
Fruit
Delicious

In the Same Boat

8:34 am Saturday
Sept 7, 2013

There are three ways that I know
Of a person's belief
Or non-belief
In God

There's the person who says
God doesn't exist
Else why does he let
Certain things happen
That shouldn't
When I would want him to appear
He doesn't

Then there's the person
Who doesn't ask God
For anything
And says God knows
What we want
Without any input
From us

And, thirdly,
The person who prays to God
And believes that
God's response rests on
His own infinite awareness
As to what's best
Under the circumstances

Really we're all in the same boat

Control

8:44 am Saturday
Sept 7, 2013

Those she loves
She controls

Those she needs
She controls

Of course,
There's justification for this

It protects
It provides

But oh the cost
When boundaries are crossed
That shouldn't be

Counterproductive

8:50 am Saturday
Sept 7, 2013

The rebellion
Against parental authority,
Against paternal authority

I'm told it has its place
Is healthy

But unresolved

Carrying over to adult life
To adult pursuits
To positions of responsibility
Can be woefully
Counterproductive

The Young

7:30 am Saturday
Sept 14, 2013

What can I say
About the young

Most obviously,
They're young

I'd rather not go
Into details

You can imagine
What they are

But I'm forced
To say
However reluctantly

That one of the
Saddest things
The Young do
Is as they grow older
They cling to the habits
The misbehaviors
The inanities
That they possessed
In their young years

It Feels Right

10:04 am Sunday
Sept 15, 2013

At long last
It feels right

I was not able
To get a doctorate
In psychology
And for good reason

Nor in English
Or history
Which would
Ultimately
Not have been the path for me

Or in politics

Wow, I would have been
Out of place
Always disagreeing
With the others

No,
Practicing counseling
Even a peritis
In the church

And all that furniture
The gardening
The church

That was right
Thanks to God

He Doesn't Belong

8:47 am Monday
Sept 16, 2013

He doesn't belong
Not really
In his own eyes
He doesn't belong

And so, he tries
To belong

Various strategies
Take your pick.

He tries harder than the rest
To excel
To succeed
Even to lead

He lies, deceives
Changes those aspects about him
To conform
To belong

And all the while
He knows
Otherwise

He would have been
Better off
Had he taken a different path

To stay himself
Be himself
Be honest
And thereby stronger
Solid
To know himself
And have others
Know him.

The Incompetency of Leadership

9:34 am Monday
Sept 16, 2013

In the beginning
There isn't much
Born, more or less,
Like others
Depending on circumstances

We are by ourselves
Or with others
We grow up
More or less

There are groups
Group settings

And things are done
Activities

And decisions
The group moves in certain directions
And needs decisions
And leaders
Or a leader

And a leader comes forth

And crisis strikes

And a decision,
Forced

And dangers still
And challenges faced
That prove,
That strengthen

A spate of dangers
Of challenges
Ongoing

And slowly
Almost deliberately
Faced

And so,
Life goes on

And leadership is handled
Differently
By those somehow
In those positions

Concealed may be a desire
To magnify oneself
And this by
Various means
Again,
Depending on circumstances

To perpetuate oneself
Seems to be most common

To stay in the leadership position
To see oneself
As worthy
Nay,
Indispensable

And all this
Despite evidence
To the contrary

The ego has taken over

Somewhat fortunately
Or semi-fortunately
There comes an end
The illusion runs its course

Unless, perhaps, we are dealing
With hereditary issues
In private or public life
And progeny are propped up
Not always inappropriately
But often

And the incompetency
Of leadership
Comes
And prevails

Challenges

3:26 pm Monday
Sept 22, 2013

Early on,
Living,
Blossoming

Forces battering
Withstood
Continually

Unrecognized
Not even understood,
Ongoing

And the horrors
The dangers
Never the less, withstood

Still unknowing

And tragedy strikes
And chaos follows

Somehow
Some way
Persisting

Protected

Glory

3:44 pm Monday
Sept 22, 2013

There is something glorious about life
Life is a glory
All its own

Lived openly,
Fully
Life is glorious

And what of a life
Lived less openly
Less freely
Hidden

What of a life lived
Silently
Hidden
Never blooming
Never shared

I say that such a life
Is surely tragic
But the tragedy of it
Has a glory all its own

The immensity of it
Is drama

God!

8:20 am Monday
Sept 30, 2013

God!
Life is so interesting
Exciting
Amazing

And the world
The earth
The air
The water
The stars
The planets

God!
How come all this

Humans
Animals
Tigers
Elephants
Cats
Dogs

God!
The wonderful things
      that man creates

And Man himself
And woman
Especially woman

West Point Prep School, 1939 Camp Dix

New Years Day 1945 in Germany

The Cathedral at Chartres August 1944

Author's wife with dog Peanuts on sand dunes at
Pismo Beach, CA

Paul's Heaven

8:20 pm Sunday
Oct. 20, 2013

I had a friend,
Paul,
Whose face was pockmarked
And who believed that
When we die
And go to heaven
Our faces would become
Clearer

And when Dotty died
Some three weeks ago
And we attended her rosary
I go up and mentioned
That for some years
She had been virtually
Out of it
Unable to respond

And when news came
That she had died
I immediately began
To think of her
As vibrant, energetic
As she had once been
Years before

This may be
Paul's heaven

If Then

8:02 am Thursday
Oct. 24, 2013

The early years
Must be like the early years
Of an amoeba
Experiencing
Without conscious awareness
Living from moment
To moment

And later comes
Awareness
Awareness and experiencing
But nothing more

And later comes experiencing
And reacting
Actively or passively

And later, perhaps,
There is realizing
Or understanding

But only much later
If then

The Gnawing

11:00 am Saturday
Nov. 2, 2013

I've been reading Thomas Merton's
Seven story mountain
And I'm at the point
Where he is visiting
Churches in Rome

And he is struck
He doesn't seem to know
By what

And he feels that he is visited
    by his father
Who has been dead a year

And he, at the time,
A non-Catholic
Describes the fear
The terror
That he says
A non-Catholic
Feels, to be praying,
Out in the open,
That is, inside a Catholic Church
To be seen by people
So doing

And his experience
Is so intense

Eventually, he does convert
To Catholicism

There are two things here
For me

Myself, a life long Catholic
I never the less
Was not a regular church goer
The first thirty years,
Really forty years
Of my life

I never, however,
Felt the powerful impact
That Merton describes

Church seemed natural to me
Church seems natural to me
The emotional, the spiritual
      feeling
Is rather a calm one
It's like home
It is home

Then there is the non-Catholic
Like Merton

Typically, his ancestors
        were Catholic
It may account for that
        ever-present
Perhaps regularly repressed,
Or suppressed,
Gnawing
Or what I am inclined to believe
Is gnawing
Maybe it goes away
Maybe it never does.

Paris is liberated, Sept. 1, 1944.

Chocolate and Cigarettes

7:35 am Wednesday
Nov 6, 2013

At breakfast this morning
My wife wondered
What has been done
With Elsie's paintings
Elsie having given up her home
To live in an assisted living facility

Which triggered a memory
From many years past
When
In the summer of 1944
In France
After the St. Lo breakthrough
We were quartered
In Le Mans

And perhaps that first day
In the morning
I found myself walking
In the town
The streets deserted

When I was approached
    by a lad
Nine or ten years old
Who asked for chocolate

As I put my hand in my pocket
(I was in uniform)
I was suddenly besieged
By seven or eight or nine
      other lads
About the same age
Clamoring for chocolate
Saying, desperately
"Je n'ai jamais avu
      du chocolat"
I emptied my pockets of the
K-ration chocolate bars
Which were of small size

That same morning I
Was in a small shop
Still in Le Mans
Where I admired a painting
A painting titled
"Le Foret de Fontaine bleu"
And we, the shop keeper and I,
Reached a bargain
And for a few packs of cigarettes
The painting, which I still have,
Was mine.

Which brings to mind
That merely a few days earlier
As we rolled through
St. Lo,
Almost completely rubble
In our tanks
And jeeps

Children, boys of eight or ten
Were asking for
Cigarettes

Jerry

8:34 am Thursday
Nov 7, 2013

Jerry was a smoker
Much too much so
One day I asked him
Jerry why don't you quit?"
"I can't" he said
And some time later
He died

A sad end
To a sad story
A very sad story

His wife had had
A hysterectomy
A year or so earlier
And died from complications

And as Jerry's children
Tried to get him out of his
Sadness
And took him to Lake Havasu,
I think,
His daughter was killed,
Instantly,
By a contraption
That one of her sons was using
On the lake,
That had gone out of control

Crazy

8:57 am Thursday
Nov 7, 2013

Most people are crazy,
More or less

This has long been known,
More or less

Maybe 150 years ago
A German psychiatrist
Made an effort
To clarify things
To systematize our knowledge
Of such matters

Paranoia,
Schizophrenia,
Paranoid schizophrenia
Manic depression
Involutional melancholia, he said

And people were put
In hospitals
For the insane

The basic issue
With such people
Is that they could not
Conduct themselves
Well enough
To manage through life

But the paranoidal patient
Is but a small percentage
Of the total population
Of paranoids, I believe

Or, for that matter,
Are manic depressives
Schizophrenics
And so on

I don't know
To what extent
This state of affairs
Contributes
To our society's
Dysfunctional state
But I bet it helps

Of course,
There are so many factors
Involved

Many of these factors
Are mild

Insufficiency of character
Of honesty
Of strength
Of courage
Of relatedness
Of concern
Etc, Etc.

That's the Story

5:12 pm Friday
Nov 8, 2013

I had planned to call
To wish him
"Happy Birthday"

Just to call him

But he called me,
A few days before
To tell me he didn't
Want me to

I had called maybe
A few weeks earlier.
I don't remember.
His wife answered
And I said, "What can you tell me?"

Anyway,
On this call,
A few days before his birthday
He referred to that call

He figured,
"Artie is up to his old tricks"
"What old tricks?"
"You want to get to know
    my family"

That I had some
Ulterior motive
In what I had said

His wife doesn't lie,
He said,
And called her to the phone
And she verified that I had
Said this strange thing

And that's the story

Chocolate and Cigarettes 54

A Square in Spain 1989,
dancers on stilts, 8 or more feet tall

Chocolate and Cigarettes 55

Leo and writer, 1989, in Spain

Leo, Leo

5:40 pm Friday
Nov 8, 2013

Leo, Leo
What happened to you?

Everything seemed quite normal
All of us rather content,
Happy

There was that time
The four of us would go to
The Holiday Inn
For those nice breakfasts
After Sunday Mass
Till that massive earthquake
Damaged the Holiday Inn
And then we went
Somewhere else, I believe

And the time you called
And wondered if I, we,
Would be interested in
A two week tour
Of Spain
And I went for it

And we had a great time
Starting with a rather adventurous
Few days in Madrid

We suddenly came upon
Some dangerous-looking men
At that outdoor bazaar
Or something. It was huge.

And trying to navigate our way
Around Madrid
With you holding the map
And guiding us

You'd had little experience
With maps

You'd spent almost a year
Based in England
With the 8th Air Force
Of the Army Air Corps
Doing bombing runs
Over Germany

You'd had an adventurous life
You'd been, I think, in Venezuela

Various construction projects

And then the first signs
Of Parkinson's

It started maybe ten years ago
I'm not sure

And the tremors
Went on for some years

And the speech

You began to have trouble
Speaking

And then you could
Hardly speak
And then you couldn't

And recognition
The signs of recognition
Began to disappear
And then it was gone

But then there was that
Brief moment
And the smile,
That smile

What I Have Done

8:10 am Monday
Dec 2, 2013

What I have done
And what I have failed to do

Aye,
There's the rub

Who knows what he has
Failed to do

And from whence
Comes the failure

I know
I know
It comes from looking
Elsewhere

When I could have invited my brother
To lunch
To talk
To advise
To clear the air

I was looking
I was thinking
Elsewhere,
Otherwise

A Pigeon

3:00 pm Monday
Nov 25, 2013

A couple of minutes ago
I was sitting in my backyard
And after a while,
A pigeon came by
And sat on a high wire
Accompanied by another one,
Probably a mate,
About twenty feet away

I have admired birds
Over the years
Flying seems like
A stupendous accomplishment
To me

And the first pigeon
Looked around
For a few minutes
And then
And then
Turned around
Right up there
On the wire

Anyway,
I am amazed

There's a Certain

7:39 am Tuesday
Dec 10, 2013

There's a certain amount
Of disbelief
In all this

Yet, there is the matter
Of faltering steps

Of weakness

Of failing eyesight

Of stooped-overness
And yet
I need to be reminded
By frailties asserting themselves

And yet
And yet
There it is

Ninety Three

It's hard to argue
With that

That's How I Would Have Done It

9:45 am Friday
Dec 13, 2013

We've just returned
From Mass

The priest was
Father Michael, a Nigerian
Who, I think,
Prefers to be known
As Father Mike

He is a great priest
He is quite popular
A tall fellow
He is bursting with energy
And faith

In that sense
He is not unlike
Other priests from Africa

For the past ten years
Or twenty, and more
We've been getting
Priests from Africa
The Philippines,
India, Vietnam

These priests from
Distant places
Seem to be rescuing us

There's been a diminution
Of vocations
From Ireland,
From our own country,
And so, these others,
Are quite welcome
They've come to the rescue

It's not as simple
As it sounds

Something miraculous
Has occurred

Not too many years back
Maybe thirty years
Certainly forty or fifty years
This would not have even
Been thought of

Colored people,
African Americans,
Blacks, were most unwelcome

Now, priests from elsewhere
Epitomize the universality
Of the Catholic Church
All well and good

But, how come, I asked myself
Today
That these two manifestations
Occurred so close together?

After all,
Vocations have tended to be
Plentiful

But for a while, not so

And how come these new arrivals
Are so plentiful
Just now

And the out pouring
Of all this acceptance

If I were God,
I tell you
That's how I would
Have done it

Learning

9:14 am Friday
Dec 27, 2013

The ways of learning
As the Christmas days
Wind down
It's set me thinking

Ways of learning
By example

Oh, there's school
Talks
Lectures
Books
Exercises

Debates too
Challenges
Questioning

By sight
By hearing
Smell
Feeling

Yes

Then there's humility
And wisdom
Learning through wisdom

Father Martin

9:24 pm Monday
Dec 30, 2013

The other day
Father Martin, a Mexican,
Strode up to where priests
Usually give their homilies
Saying
"I want to talk about
Pope Francis"
An unusual beginning

And I suppose what followed
Had to do with
 The Pope

All I remember is
Three words
"Bitterness", "submission"
And "tolerance"

A laudable focus,
Really

First, bitterness

He noted that bitterness
Can destroy a person
From inside
Can destroy a person's life

In this long life of mine
I've seen the truth of this
It must be hard to get rid of
Bitterness
And I've seen it take over
And contaminate a person's
Vital force
His spirit

And it may go undetected
Because a person is capable
Of having many faces

And, then
Submission
Submission to the realities
Of life
Submission to God's will
Submission that allows
Freedom
Paradoxical as that may seem

To battle always
To distrust
Almost universally
Puts one in a corner
Of estrangement
Of non-participation
Even as life goes on

And then,
Tolerance
A laudable attitude
In our culture
It seems innocent enough

But then we can tolerate
To the point of destruction
Of our values
Our life-giving structures

Marriage, for instance
Anything goes

And then the very pillars
Of a healthy, happy society
A respecting society

We don't need tolerance
As much as we need
Mercy
And truth

Chocolate and Cigarettes 69

Cross Country Trip, 1948

Islam

9:42 pm Monday
Dec 30, 2013

I could very well
Be mistaken
You tell me

Once, many years ago
I read some lines
In the Koran
Which said something like
"Kill all infidels"

Most Muslims say
No, it's not so
Islam is a religion
Of peace
Of brotherhood
Only a few
A small minority
Do these things
They do not have the
True spirit
Of Islam

Yet, worldwide
Such goes on

Wherever,
However

Maybe ten churches
Burned to the ground
In one day

And, more than once
The slaughter of
Whole congregations
By burning a church
With services,
With Mass,
Going on

And the slaughter of those
Trying to escape

We're innocent they say
And slaughters, the bombings
The denials continue

Heroically

4:55 pm Wednesday
Jan 8, 2014

It happened so long ago
Nineteen forty nine perhaps
We were driving west
From New York to California
At night

Maybe Route 66
Dark
No lights
Except for the headlights
On our bedraggled Buick

We had been married
Maybe two years
We were having
Those various adventures
Of the young

When out of the darkness
The blackness of that night
We saw a car
Coming from the opposite direction
The west
Hit what was probably
A truck tire on the road

And that car
Went soaring up
Into the air
Maybe twenty feet

And landed maybe
Another twenty feet away
Landing, I discovered,
As I stopped our car
And faced it toward
Where the other car had landed
And trained my headlights
On the scene

Within minutes
Ten or twenty men,
Miraculously,
Converged on the scene

And one of the men,
Said that a train was due
In six minutes
And then, together,
We, heroically,
Lifted the car off the tracks

Will I?

10:50 am Saturday
Jan 11, 2014

This morning at breakfast
I found my self
Thinking of my Mom
And would I get to see her
Again

And, my wife,
As she is wont to do
Said that I would,
Especially with certain prayers
To the Virgin

And, my Dad
Him too
We'd been through so much
Together

Will I?
Will we?

Mine

11:28 am, Wednesday
Jan 15, 2014

When I was younger
When I was a young man,
That is
I would on occasion
Hear the phrase
"This woman is mine"
And so I believed

But, somewhat older now
And experienced
And long married
I learned that the phrase
Has a twist to it

Woman buys the phrase
And proceeds to take over

All women
In my experience
Seem to subscribe

Our Little Acre

3:00 pm Sunday
Jan 19, 2014

Our little acre
We've lived here
Fifty six years

It is not an acre
Really
More like a quarter of an acre

But I like to call it that
Just now

I've just been doing
Some gardening
Planting two new trees
An apricot and a fig

Makes twelve fruit-bearing
Trees

Plus ten Hollywood Junipers
Out front

I like all this
I'd never owned a home
Before
Growing up

The Other Day

8:44 am Wednesday
Jan 29, 2014

The other day
An 82-year-old woman
Who I've known
For half her life
Told me

That after calling me
And a number of her friends
And relatives
Repeatedly,
Day and night

Asking for our counsel
Our sympathy
Our prayers

To help mitigate
Or banish
Her fears
Her scruples
Her demons

All of us trying
Patiently
To help

That one of these friends,
 Joannie,
Her age
Having died
A few days ago
And scheduled to be buried
This Friday
May have had some connection
To an unusual
Manifestation
A bright light
Encompassing
A large area in front of her
As she was driving

It was very bright
And it was not frightening
It was, in fact,
Comforting,
It did not interfere
With her driving

It was God
A friend of hers said

The Tribunal

6:00 am Tuesday
Feb 4, 2014

It's hard to believe
No, it's not

That God reaches out

Why not?

That He is present

But it is truly
Hard to believe

And in dreams
As he seems to have done
To me

Just minutes ago
Priests and others
Re-playing
Or trying to
Tribunal days
And I was a peritus
Still am
According to Moretti
My good friend, Gus

Suddenly, in this dream
It seems to have been re-played
That incident
In 1975
Thirty eight or nine years ago
A noon time nap
In my office on Ventura Blvd
Awakening with the thought
That there should be more
To this
To this life

And referring this back
To the knowledge
That an annulment talk
Was to be given that evening
At St. Joseph's hospital
In Burbank
By Mgr. Cliff Parker

And we went
My wife and I

And I called the next day
To volunteer
A volunteering that went on
For ten years

And remarkable things occurred
With my having little
Or no knowledge of them
Till later,
That a new and blessed transformation
Began to occur
And did occur

Disguises

10:05 am Wednesday
Feb 5, 2014

We live at a time
When support is lacking
The kind that counts

We live separated lives
No longer bolstered
Instructed
Encouraged
By kin

No longer trained,
Restrained,
By loving arms

And government structures
Benevolent entities
Cannot do
What truly works

And evil abounds
Abounds in many forms
Usually wearing disguises

The Eternal

9:26 am Saturday
Feb 8, 2014

I'm not interested
In your status
Your income
Your career

All I'm interested in is
Your well-being
Your happiness
Your integrity

These other things
Prized in these,
Our times . . .
Fool's gold

They are more ephemeral
Than you know

And these others
The joyful
The honorable
Now, there,
There we have solidity,
Permanence . . . the eternal

A Form of Expression

10:04 am Saturday
Feb 8, 2014

There is that kind
Of situation
That develops well
Develops gloriously, even

And this can sometimes
Continue for quite a while

Sometimes over a period of years
Even centuries

And somehow
It doesn't last forever
In human terms
It is corrupted

And the good still existing
Within
Must either be quashed
Or find some form
Of expression

Within
Or without

Underlying

9:27 am Monday
Feb 10, 2014

There's that issue
Of self to self

Who am I?
Who are you?

What do you
Or I
Stand for

Good Pope Francis
A month or two ago
When asked about gays
Astonished many by saying
"Who am I to judge?"

There must be a lot of
All sorts of pressure
On a pope
To uphold
The established protocol
Not to reveal
The humility
The honesty
The humanness
Underlying

An Inner Force

7:30 am Tuesday
Feb 18, 2014

This morning
At breakfast
Just a few minutes ago
As I was having herring
With cream cheese
On a slice of bread

I was reminded
Of a bar mitzvah
Where I'd first encountered
This pleasant food
Some ten or more
Years ago

And of the father of the boy
Whose transition
Was being celebrated

I had known him
Since his infancy

And, of late,
He has become large
Overweight
Obese

And I wonder
How come?

Over the years
I have witnessed
Persons driven
Driven by some inner force

All else ignored
Neglected

It seems to be
An inner force
But, it cannot be an inner force,
Originally

No, it must be something
That enters from without
Striking with such force
Gradually,
Or in an instant
That pierces the heart

The Chess Board

6:21 am Friday
Feb 21, 2014

It seems that life
Is like a chess board

If you wish to advance
You must secure
The space before

If you wish
Merely to manage
The issues
The trials of life
You must have
The where-with-all
To do it

And if you wish
To live this life
You will face obstacles

And obstacles come
They will come
In many forms

This is Too Much

10:30 am Tuesday
Mar 4, 2014

A little while ago, my son,
Who lives in Texas
Called to tell me
That his dog, Rex,
Was dying
That he'd been, my son,
That is
Up with him all night

Having been pretty much
Without sleep
Through the night
Plus, staying with his dog
Means not going in to work
Today

And, last night,
Our other son who lives
All the way up in San Luis
Brought us up to date
On his plans to re-enter
The home-owning world

Yesterday, we continued our efforts
To switch banks
An effort complicated somewhat
By one of the banks
The one we're leaving
Suddenly becoming unresponsive

An appropriate thing, perhaps,
For as I was driving, my brakes
Seemed to be unresponsive
As well

And the ceiling light fixtures
In the library
Need to be replaced

And the new fig tree
Was water-logged
Due to the heavy rains
And needs to be rescued

And the car, not ready yet

This is too much
I'm 93
For God's sake

Misfittings

9:25 am Saturday
Mar 8, 2014

This morning
At breakfast
As is usual
My wife and I
Discussed some things
People

That some people
Too many
Have a constricted
View of life

For instance

I've become aware
That a person can view others
As being pretty much the same
And all possessing
Certain qualities

Or as being,
Somewhere out there
All of them

Maybe in certain
Categories

And some such people
Never marry
For various reasons
And so maintain
The aforementioned
Perspective
Untrammeled

But some there are
Who do marry
And hold on to such

And negative they are

And there is a misfitting
With or without marriage
And throughout their lives
These misfittings
Continue

You Know

10:04 pm Saturday
Mar 8, 2014

You know,
Getting married is
A unique kind of thing
A unique experience

I realize that
Billions of people
Get married
But, still, it would seem
That each such action
Is unique
As indeed
Each of us is

You learn that the
Person you marry
Is unique,
From all the rest
Of his or her sex
Is different
Special, even

Knowingly or not
Consciously or not
Marriage entails
A surrender

Each person puts himself
In the others hands
For life,
One way or another

There's no way out of it

And from such a perspective
You deal with issues
Accordingly

Getting married, really,
Ideally
Requires, courage, honesty
Commitment,
The ability to love
The ability to endure

Without these
You have a problem

Nowadays, increasingly
Couples are chancing marriage
They think,
Without getting married

The marriage commitment
May be too daunting
Too risky
So that simply getting into
A relationship which
Doesn't require the
Aforementioned qualities
Is simply, safer
Not to mention modern
More in keeping with the times
And nobody gets hurt

Wrong, horribly wrong
The waste of time
Though obvious
Is only one thing

But the other wastes

Incalculable

God Loves You

12:24 pm Sunday
Mar 9, 2014

Really,
I can see how you feel
If I can be permitted
This conjecture
For it is no simple thing
For one person to feel another person's pain

And your situation
Is not a happy one

For no-one ventures
On the journey of marriage
Anticipating what you
Have experienced

The husband you love
Was harsh
And still you loved him
And three, four or five years ago
He had this cruelly disabling
Stroke
And still you loved him

And your three sons
One in prison for years
Another on disabling drugs
The third a disabled neurotic
No prizes there

And your daughter
Having to find her way
Unable to provide you
With help
Or with inspiring progeny
No,
She has her hands full

And, here,
I don't want to
Or intend to
Be patronizing

You are an amazing woman
Your load is heavy
But you are strong

You take care of everyone
You are able

The many people you
Take care of
Should provide you
With a clue

You are healthy, you
Have faith
You are admired

I love you
We love you

You do have a support system

God is watching over you
God loves you

Overwork

8:45 am Tuesday
Mar 11, 2014

On PBS radio this morning
There was this item
Of work
Of portioning out work
Of duties
In a marriage
And family

Primarily, the overworked woman
A mother who has
A career

That is, outside the home

And the children

And it seems that
All these facets
Requires
Nay, demands
Time, attention, effort

And it seems to boil down to
Priorities

And to what should be done
Could be done
Must be done

And the husband's
The father's work
His responsibilities

It seems to me
That in our current civilization
We are over committed
That our roles,
Our commitments, etc
Have greatly enlarged
Without our capabilities
Our resources, being
Commensurately so

There is a gross
Imbalance here

But, lest you be
Misled
There is a much larger
Elephant in this room

There are vast numbers
Of people
Without something to do
Who have no work
No jobs.

This, among the largest
Of issues
The lack of work
The lack of the ennobling
Role of work
Of an occupation
Of a goal-setting
Of an enriching
Of a stabilizing way to live

And this all goes unheeded
Disregarding,
The idiotic approaches
To solve the problem
On the part of those who have
Policy-making roles

But, truly, it is, after all
Too large a problem
For mere humans
As we know them
To deal with
While we moan over
The overburdened nature
Of our lives

But, it can be done

On the North Shore of Long Island
2009

On Normandy, France
June / July 1944

Previous Books By the Author

Unlike the Vikings

Casta Diva

Grandma and the Miracles

The Bird and the Squirrel

Rosalie Was All Night Without the Light

Rivershore Books

Website:
www.rivershorebooks.com

Blog:
blog.rivershorebooks.com

Facebook:
www.facebook.com/rivershore.books

Twitter:
www.twitter.com/rivershorebooks

Email:
Jansina@rivershorebooks.com

Printed in Great Britain
by Amazon